101 THINGS® TO DO WITH A

101 THINGS® TO DO WITH A

STEVE TILLETT

Gibbs Smith

Second Edition
28 27 26 25 24   5 4 3 2 1

First Gibbs Smith edition published in 2005
Second Gibbs Smith edition published February 2024

Published by
Gibbs Smith
P.O. Box 667
Layton, Utah 84041

1.800.835.4993 orders
www.gibbs-smith.com

Designed by Ryan Thomann and Renee Bond
Printed and bound in China
Gibbs Smith books are printed on either recycled, 100% post-consumer
waste, FSC-certified papers or on paper produced from sustainable PEFC-
certified forest/controlled wood source. Learn more at www.pefc.org.

The Library of Congress has cataloged the first edition as follows:

Tillett, Steve.
101 things to do with a BBQ / Steve Tillett.—1st ed.
p. cm.
ISBN 1-58685-698-7 (first edition)
1. Barbecue cookery. I. Title.
TX840.B3T554 2005
641.5'784—dc22   2004021117
ISBN: 978-1-4236-6560-1

This book is dedicated to Suzanne Taylor, whose vision helped bring this book to fruition, and to my father the butcher, who taught me to BBQ and has always inspired me to accomplish anything I want to achieve. Also, to my beautiful wife and best friend, Sharon (queen of the kitchen), and to my children, Chris, Andie, Kittie, and Matthew, who have survived my many BBQ experiments, and are still willing to be my honorable taste testers. And finally, to my friends Stephanie Lamberson, Tiffany Felt, Jennifer Waldrip, the salmon king Jeff Tillett, G-ma Tillett, Grandma Barbara Gibbs, my little friend Coach Solomona Tapasa, Janice Horschel, Jennifer Pfleiger, and others who contributed their favorite family recipes to this collection.

CONTENTS

#70–82 Pork

#83–92 Seafood

#93–101 Desserts

Bonus Section
Sauces & Rubs

Helpful Hints

● Grilling "low and slow" is the often-heard adage and barbecue mantra. If you say "cook it low and slow" to a grill enthusiast, their response, usually accompanied by a grin, is, "Yep, low and slow."

- The goal with grilling low and slow is to avoid the intense heat that dries the meat out; the outside becomes too well-done and the juices are lost along with their flavor. Ideally, you can set up the grill to cook via indirect heat. This can be done by using a second, or a top shelf, turning off part of the gas grill to create a cooler area, or even covering part of the grate with heavy-duty aluminum foil.

- No matter how you do it, the concept is the same; you are modifying the cooking area to be more indirect, much like an oven. The advantages of this method will help the meat you are grilling remain moist and flavorful, and you typically don't need to turn the meat as often. The meat cooks more evenly throughout, and you avoid the charring or burning caused from direct flames.

- Still, is there an appropriate time to grill "hot and fast?" Here is the long-of-the-short, or the short-of-the-long, answer my father "Big Red" Ron Tillett, the butcher, used to give: "Crank the heat for the thinner cut of meat. For a thicker cut, take a seat on your butt."

● The internal temperature of a cooked cut of meat not only defines safe cooking, but determines how tender, juicy, and flavorful it will be. The best way to improve your grilling skills is to invest in a good digital instant-read meat thermometer. This will take the guesswork out of trying to determine if the meat is done to your liking, or cooked to a recommended safe temperature to help avoid foodborne illness.

- It is best to baste the barbecue sauce on when the meat is done cooking. If you apply barbecue sauce to your meat before it is done, it will most assuredly burn. You're not trying to cook the sauce. However, a nice trick is to heat the sauce prior to applying it to the meat. Once you apply the sauce, it takes no more than a minute or two to get the sauce to set up (glazed over) and hold onto the skin.

- Turn meat with tongs, instead of a fork, so you limit the loss of natural juices from puncturing the meat.

- Boil leftover marinade in a saucepan over high heat. This kills any bacteria left by raw meat and makes it safe to use for basting during the last 5 minutes of grilling, or as a warm sauce for the finished dish.

- Liquid smoke used in small amounts is a great way to make your food taste like it spent all day in the smoker.

- Smoking foods on a gas grill is easy. The only things needed are wood chips and a smoker box. Pick up smoker wood chips from a local sporting goods store. Apple, cherry, hickory, or mesquite chips work well for pork, beef, or poultry. Try alder for fish.

- If you don't own a smoker box or don't want to buy one, smoker pouches are easy to make. Follow these simple instructions:
  - Use a large piece of heavy-duty aluminum foil, about 12 inches long. Place wood chips in the middle and wrap securely. Poke holes in top of pouch with a meat thermometer and it's ready to go. For large cuts of meat such as roasts, place the wood chips in water and soak for 30 minutes to 2 hours then place wood chips in smoker pouch. For smaller cuts of meat, dry chips are fine.
  - Place your smoker pouch under the grilling grate, directly over the flame. Turn grill to high heat until smoke begins to rise from the pouch. Immediately turn grill down to desired cooking temperature and cook your food at the appropriate temperature, letting the wood chips go to work.

- Meat becomes more tender when cooked slowly at a low temperature, no matter how high the grade. Also, meat served hot is usually more tender than meat served cold.

- As a general rule, use approximately 1½ cups of marinade for every 1 to 2 pounds of meat. Make sure it completely covers the meat. Let your meat marinate in a large ziplock bag in the refrigerator. Double bag to prevent leaks. You can also freeze marinating meats for future uses.

- Marinade is the quickest way to tenderize meat and add additional zest. A quick 30-minute marinate will give meat a great taste. Marinating even longer will give you more flavor. When marinating in the refrigerator, remove meat and let it come to room temperature before grilling.

- To help prevent your food from sticking, spray the grill grate with cooking spray, or wipe with oil prior to grilling. This will also make it easier to clean the grill once you're done.

- To clean the grill after using, lay a piece of aluminum foil over the grate, shiny side down, and turn to high heat for 5 minutes. This will burn off any buildup on the grates. Watch the grill closely and do not leave unattended. When the 5 minutes are up, gently brush the grate with a wire brush.

- For a grill that needs some serious cleaning, try using 2 tablespoons of baking soda added to 1 cup water. Brush it on with your wire brush, let sit for 2–3 minutes, and then scrub with the wire brush.

Advanced Grilling Tips

BEEF

🥄 Cook beef according to taste for the amount of time shown below.

Thickness	Doneness	Grilling Time Per Side
1 inch	rare	3–4 minutes
	medium	5–7 minutes
1½ inches	rare	5–7 minutes
	medium	8–9 minutes
2 inches	rare	7–9 minutes
	medium	9–11 minutes

🥄 Cook roast according to taste for the amount of time and temperature shown below.

Rare	140 degrees	20 minutes per pound
Medium	160 degrees	25 minutes per pound
Well	170 degrees	30 minutes per pound

🥄 To barbecue, turn grill to high heat, approximately 450 degrees F. The hotter the grill, the better it will seal in the juices. Place beef on grate and sear 30–60 seconds on each side, using tongs to turn so the natural juices stay sealed. Turn grill down to medium and finish cooking according to taste and desired doneness. Turn meat several times throughout total grilling time.

POULTRY

- The trick to grilling chicken is to do it slowly and turn it frequently. Approximate cooking time is 20–30 minutes for chicken breasts, tenders, or thighs, and 20 minutes per pound if chicken is whole.

- When cooking chicken with skin on, put a layer of heavy-duty aluminum foil on the bottom grate of the grill and cook the chicken on the middle or top rack. This will reduce the flare-ups and decrease the chance of burning.

- To check if chicken is cooked through, squeeze it. When the juices run clear it is probably done. Double-check by using an instant-read thermometer placed into the thickest portion of the meat, making sure not to touch any bone. The temperature should be 165 degrees F.

- To thaw frozen chicken, remove from freezer and place in the refrigerator the day before use. If in a hurry or for same-day use, place chicken in a bowl and fill with cool water. Allow to soak until thawed. Change water every few minutes to speed up the process.

PORK

- The guidelines for safely preparing pork have changed, and now recommend pork to be cooked to an internal temperature of 145 degrees F, followed by a 5 minute rest time.

- Pork is naturally drier than other meats. Do not to overcook it. Approximate cooking time is 30–35 minutes per pound. Using an instant-read thermometer will alleviate the guess work.

- Marinades and brines will add a lot of flavor while helping to moisten your pork.

SEAFOOD

- When grilling fish, do not turn it, and quickly remove it from grill when it is no longer opaque. Do not overcook.

- Rubbing the grate with oil will help keep the fish from sticking.

- Leave scales on bigger fish and cook scale side down. Salmon on the grill is best cooked on top of aluminum foil.

- Grill trout over low but direct heat to add a hearty smoked flavor.

- Other fish, like swordfish, tuna, mackerel, and bluefish, are great choices for grilling because their natural oils help keep them moist and flaky.

- Thicker fillets stand up to the heat of the grill better than thin ones.

- Using a grill basket or aluminum foil for thinner fillets of fish can keep it from falling apart.

#1-8

APPETIZERS

Grilled Summer Veggies

MAKES 3–5 SERVINGS

1	**medium zucchini**
1	**large red bell pepper**
1 pound	**fresh asparagus**
1 pound	**cherry tomatoes**
1/4 cup	**olive oil, plus more if needed**
	salt and freshly ground pepper, favorite seasoning salt, or Steve's Famous Dry Rub (page 119), to taste

Preheat grill to medium low.

Wash the vegetables and pat dry with paper towels. Cut the zucchini and bell pepper into 1/2-inch-thick slices or wedges. Cut the woody ends off of the asparagus and leave the tomatoes whole.

Place vegetables in a large bowl and drizzle oil sparingly over top. Add the seasoning and toss gently to coat. Place vegetables in a grill basket* and place basket on the grill. Cook, turning every 3–4 minutes, until done to your liking.

These grilled vegetables are great served hot off the grill with a side of ranch dressing, or chilled and served as a cold side or in place of a green salad.

*If you don't have a grill basket, fold a long piece of heavy-duty aluminum foil in half and fold up the edges to create a tray.

Caesar Salad

MAKES 2–4 SERVINGS

	olive oil
2 to 4	hearts of romaine lettuce
10 to 12	small asparagus spears or 12 Brussels sprouts
3 tablespoons	freshly grated Parmesan cheese
	Homemade Croutons (page 37)
1	fresh lemon, sliced
	freshly ground pepper, to taste
1 bottle	Caesar salad dressing, of choice

Preheat grill to medium high and lightly oil grate.

Wash and pat dry the lettuce and cut in half lengthwise. If the heads of lettuce are loose and coming apart, you can tie them gently together with kitchen twine (moisten the twine with water after tying to ensure it does not burn). Brush cut sides with oil and grill until starting to caramelize, about 2 minutes. Remove from grill and set aside.

Wash and trim the woody ends of the asparagus, if using. Place in a shallow dish and toss with a small amount of oil to coat. Do the same for the Brussels sprouts, if using. Place asparagus or sprouts in a grill basket to prevent from falling through the grate, and cook until they start to soften and caramelize a bit, 5–10 minutes.

Place two halves of the grilled romaine hearts on each individual serving plate and evenly divide the asparagus or sprouts, cheese, croutons, and lemon slices over the top. Garnish with pepper and serve with dressing on the side.

Grilled Stuffed Peppers

MAKES 4–6 SERVINGS

4 to 6	medium or large sweet bell peppers, any color
1½ cups	crushed croutons
1 cup	finely chopped sweet onion
½ cup	grated Parmesan cheese
1 tablespoon	minced garlic
1 tablespoon	finely chopped cilantro
	salt and pepper, to taste

Preheat grill to medium.

Clean and core peppers. Mix croutons, sweet onion, Parmesan cheese, garlic, and cilantro in a bowl. Scoop and pack mixture into hollowed centers of peppers. Place peppers on grill and cook for 15 minutes. Season with salt and pepper.

Poppin' BBQ Popcorn

MAKES 3–5 CUPS POPPED POPCORN

¼ cup	popcorn kernels
⅛ cup	vegetable oil
1 to 2 tablespoons	butter, melted
	Steve's Famous Dry Rub (page 119)

Preheat grill to high.

Cover bottom of a large and deep saucepan (with ovenproof handles) with a single layer of popcorn kernels. Pour oil over top of kernels. Place saucepan, covered, on grill over high heat until the popcorn begins to pop. Start to gently shake the pan, continuing until popcorn is completely popped, 3–6 minutes.

Transfer to a serving bowl and drizzle popcorn with melted butter, stirring as you drizzle. Sprinkle desired amount of dry rub over popcorn and stir again to mix well.

Parmesan Potato Wedges

MAKES 4–6 SERVINGS

4	medium potatoes, cut lengthwise into ¼-inch-thick wedges
2 tablespoons	olive oil
4 tablespoons	freshly grated Parmesan cheese
	salt and freshly ground pepper or favorite seasoning salt, to taste
	ranch dressing or dipping sauce, of choice

Preheat grill to medium.

Place potato wedges in a large ziplock bag, add oil, cheese, and salt and pepper. Seal the bag and gently toss to coat potatoes.

Remove potatoes from the bag and place in a grill basket, or lay directly on the grill across the grates so they won't fall through. Grill, turning every 3–4 minutes, until desired tenderness. Remove from grill and serve warm with a side of ranch dressing or favorite dipping sauce.

Tiffany's Cuban Potatoes
MAKES 4–6 SERVINGS

3 pounds	**potatoes (sweet or Yukon are good here)**
2 to 3 tablespoons	**olive oil**
	salt and pepper, to taste
3 to 4	**garlic cloves, minced**
1 to 3 tablespoons	**fresh lime juice**
1½ tablespoons	**chopped fresh parsley**

Preheat grill to medium high.

Slice potatoes lengthwise into ¼- to ⅛-inch-thick slices.
Toss potatoes in bowl with olive oil and season with salt and pepper. Grill until tender, 20–30 minutes. Cool on a wire rack for 15 minutes.

Transfer to a large bowl and toss with garlic, lime juice, and parsley. If potatoes appear dry, add more olive oil and season with salt and pepper again.

Blue Cheese–Stuffed Mushrooms

MAKES 4–6 SERVINGS

1 pound	fresh mushrooms, stems removed
5 ounces	blue cheese or feta
¼ cup	olive oil

Fill mushroom caps with crumbled cheese. Preheat grill to medium high, and lightly oil grate.

Place mushrooms, cheese side up, onto grill. Do not turn mushrooms over. Cook until cheese melts and mushrooms are tender.

Stuffed Tomatoes

MAKES 3–5 SERVINGS

4 to 6	medium or large tomatoes
2 cups	crushed croutons
1 cup	finely chopped sweet onion
1 tablespoon	minced garlic
1 tablespoon	finely chopped cilantro
	salt and pepper, to taste

Preheat grill to medium.

Partially core tomatoes. Mix croutons, sweet onion, garlic, and cilantro in a bowl. Scoop and pack mixture into hollowed centers of tomatoes. Place tomatoes on grill and cook for 10 minutes. Season with salt and pepper.

VEGETABLES

#9

Spicy Italian Veggies

MAKES 3–5 SERVINGS

4	Roma tomatoes
1	large red onion
2	medium yellow squash
2	green bell peppers
¼ cup	Italian salad dressing, or to taste
2 teaspoons	dried basil
	salt and freshly ground pepper, to taste

Preheat grill to medium high.

Cut the vegetables into ½-inch-thick slices or wedges. Place in a large bowl and add the dressing, tossing gently to coat. Place coated vegetable pieces in a grill basket, peel side down, and sprinkle with basil and salt and pepper. Grill 4–6 minutes, or until heated through. Do not turn.

Variation: For a spicier version, marinate vegetables in dressing for up to 6 hours.

Butter and Garlic Vegetables

MAKES 6–8 SERVINGS

2	medium zucchini
1	medium yellow squash
3	pattypan squash
2	red bell peppers
1 pound	fresh asparagus
1 pound	fresh mushrooms
4 tablespoons	melted butter
1 teaspoon	minced garlic
	seasoning salt or salt and freshly ground pepper, to taste

Preheat grill to medium high.

Cut the zucchini, squashes, and peppers into ¼- to ½-inch-thick slices or wedges and place all the vegetables in a large bowl.

In a small bowl, mix together the butter and garlic, then pour over the vegetables and toss to coat. Place vegetables in a grill basket and cook until tender, 5–10 minutes, depending on the thickness of the vegetables, and turning every 1–2 minutes. Check individual vegetables for tenderness and remove from heat to a serving dish when cooked as desired. Sprinkle with seasoning salt, or salt and pepper, and serve.

Grilled Squash and Onions

MAKES 3–5 SERVINGS

2 to 3	small zucchini
2 to 3	small yellow squash
2	small purple onions, peeled
¼ cup	olive oil, plus more if needed
2 teaspoons	garlic powder
1 teaspoon	lemon juice
	salt and freshly ground pepper, to taste

Preheat grill to medium high.

Cut the vegetables into ¼- to ½-inch-thick slices or wedges. In a small bowl, combine the oil, garlic powder, and lemon juice; mix well. Place vegetables in a large bowl, pour mixture over top, and toss to coat.

Turn the grill down to medium low and place vegetables in a grill basket. Place on the grill grate and cook for 4–6 minutes, or until tender, turning every minute or so. Sprinkle with salt and pepper.

Corn on the Cob

MAKES 6 SERVINGS

6 ears	**corn in their husks**
1 stick	**butter, softened**
	salt and freshly ground pepper, to taste

Preheat grill to medium high.

Cut off the corn silk at ends of husks and discard. Place corn on rack, close the lid, and cook, turning frequently, for 15–20 minutes, or until kernels are tender when pierced. Remove from grill.

When cool enough to handle, remove husks and any remaining corn silk. Serve with butter and salt and pepper.

Variation: Brush a light coat of mayonnaise over cooked corn and sprinkle with freshly grated Parmesan cheese.

Cabbage on the Grill

MAKES 6 SERVINGS

1	**large head cabbage**
	butter, to taste
2 teaspoons	**onion powder or salt**
	salt and freshly ground
	pepper, to taste

Preheat grill to medium and lightly oil grate.

Cut cabbage into four to eight wedges and remove core. Place wedges on a piece of heavy-duty aluminum foil large enough to wrap and completely cover cabbage. Dot wedges with pats of butter, sprinkle with onion powder, season with salt and pepper, and seal foil tightly; place directly on grill grate. Grill for 30 minutes, or until tender.

#14

Grilled Acorn Squash

MAKES 2–4 SERVINGS

2 **acorn squash**
  butter, to taste
  salt and pepper, to taste

Preheat grill to medium.

Wrap each squash individually in heavy-duty aluminum foil with a pat of butter. Place on grill grate, close lid, and cook for 20–30 minutes, or until tender.

Remove from grill and slice squash in half lengthwise; scoop out any seeds and strings.

Place the halves back on the grill, cut side up. Add another two to three pats of butter directly on top of the squash and let cook for 5–10 more minutes, or until butter is mostly absorbed.

Remove from grill, season with salt and pepper, and serve.

Variation: Slice each of the squash halves into 1-inch wedges and place back on the grill until light grill marks appear.

Grilled Asparagus

MAKES 4 SERVINGS

1 pound	**thick asparagus spears**
1 to 2 tablespoons	**olive oil**
	salt and freshly ground pepper, Steve's Famous Dry Rub (page 119), or garlic salt, to taste

Preheat grill to medium high.

Remove the woody ends of the asparagus by cutting with a knife or bending stalks until they snap, leaving the greener, tender portions of the stalk. Rinse well with water and pat dry with paper towels.

Place asparagus in a large ziplock bag, add oil and seasoning of choice, and gently massage bag to evenly coat asparagus. Remove from bag and lay the asparagus spears crosswise on grill so they won't fall through the grate, or place in a grill basket. Grill, turning every 2–3 minutes, to desired tenderness.

Steve's Heavenly Sautéed Sweet Onions

MAKES 2–4 SERVINGS

2 teaspoons	**minced garlic**
2 tablespoons	**butter**
1 to 2	**large sweet onions, chopped**
¼ cup	**grated Parmesan cheese**
	salt and pepper or
	seasoning salt, to taste

Preheat grill to medium high.

Place frying pan or flat plate directly on lower rack. Sauté garlic in butter 1 minute. Add onions and sauté 5–8 minutes, or until tender. Add Parmesan cheese and sauté 1 minute more. Season with salt and pepper.

This recipe is great over anything grilled!

Garlic Baked Potatoes

MAKES 6 SERVINGS

6	**large russet potatoes**
6 tablespoons	**butter, softened**
	garlic salt, to taste
	suggested toppings: butter, sour cream, salt and pepper, chopped green onions, grated cheese, bacon crumbles, ranch dressing, salsa, or grilled vegetables

Preheat grill to medium high.

Scrub the potatoes and then poke several times with a fork. Completely cover each potato with a thin coating of butter and sprinkle evenly with garlic salt.

Place potatoes on grill grate out of direct heat. Close lid and bake 40–50 minutes, or until potatoes are tender when pierced, turning a couple of times during cooking. Serve with favorite toppings.

BREADS, SANDWICHES & PIZZA

Greek Pastry Pizza

MAKES 4–6 SERVINGS

¼ cup	**olive oil**
¼ teaspoon	**salt**
2 to 4 teaspoons	**minced fresh garlic, or to taste**
1 loaf	**French, ciabatta, or focaccia bread**

Toppings:

1 cup	**grated mozzarella cheese**
2	**Roma tomatoes, sliced**
¼ to ½ cup	**artichoke hearts**
¼ cup	**black or Kalamata olives, halved**
2	**green onions, sliced**
2 ounces	**crumbled feta cheese**
2 tablespoons	**chopped fresh basil**

Preheat grill to medium high.

Combine oil, salt, and garlic together in a small bowl. Cut the bread in half and then cut each half lengthwise. Brush garlic mixture evenly over the cut side of each piece of bread. Carefully place bread halves cut side down on the grill and toast for 1–2 minutes, or until it begins to brown. Remove from grill.

Divide topping ingredients evenly and layer over the toasted side of each piece of bread in order listed. Return the prepared bread to the grill, close lid, and continue to cook for 2–4 minutes, or until the bottom starts to brown and the cheese has melted. If cheese is slow to melt, move the bread to upper rack of the grill and close the lid. Check every 1–2 minutes until done. If the grill does not have an upper rack, place the pizzas on a couple of sheets of heavy-duty aluminum foil to prevent the bottom from burning while cheese melts.

> Variation: For a thin crust, scoop out the middle of the cut bread pieces and fill with the toppings and cheese.

#19

Grilled Garlic Bread

MAKES 3–5 SERVINGS

1 loaf	French or Italian bread
4 tablespoons	butter, softened
1 to 2 tablespoons	minced fresh garlic or garlic salt, or to taste
½ cup	freshly grated Parmesan cheese

Preheat grill to low.

Cut bread in half lengthwise. Place cut side down on grill and lightly toast. Remove bread from grill and set aside. In a small bowl, mix together the butter, garlic, and Parmesan cheese until well combined. Spread mixture on toasted side of bread. Place bread back on the grill out of direct heat, buttered side up. Close the lid and cook until the cheese mixture is hot and melted.

Pizza Bites

MAKES 2 PIZZAS

	olive oil
2 (12-inch)	premade pizza crusts
1 tablespoon	extra virgin olive oil, divided
2 cups	crushed tomatoes or favorite pizza sauce, divided
2 to 3 cups	freshly grated mozzarella, divided
	pizza toppings such as: pepperoni, prosciutto, salami, Canadian bacon, cooked sausage, cooked bacon crumbles, olives, tomato slices, fresh mushrooms, artichoke hearts, roasted red or yellow bell peppers, or sliced green onions
¼ cup	minced fresh rosemary, fresh basil leaves, torn into small pieces, or fresh oregano leaves, divided, optional
	freshly grated Parmesan cheese, optional

Preheat grill to medium high.

Using tongs, dip a folded paper towel in olive oil and rub over the grill grates.

Brush the top of each pizza crust lightly with ½ tablespoon olive oil and spread 1 cup of crushed tomatoes or pizza sauce evenly over the top to within ½ inch of the edge. Sprinkle 1 to 1½ cups of mozzarella over the sauce and add two to three of your favorite toppings (you don't want to overload the pizza).

Carefully slide pizzas onto the grill grates out of direct heat, close the lid, and cook for 5–10 minutes, or until the cheese melts, checking often to make sure the bottom doesn't burn. If the bottom is getting too dark, but the toppings still need more time to heat or melt, lower the heat, place the pizzas on a couple of pieces of heavy-duty aluminum foil or a pizza stone, close the lid, and continue to cook, checking every 2 minutes. When cooked to liking, remove pizzas from the grill and transfer to a cutting board. Sprinkle tops with fresh herbs and Parmesan cheese. Cut into small wedges or squares and serve with a side salad for a light lunch.

#21

Homemade Croutons

MAKES 6–8 SERVINGS

1 loaf	day-old French bread
½ cup	olive or vegetable oil
1 to 2 tablespoons	garlic powder, or to taste
2 tablespoons	dried sweet basil

Preheat grill to medium.

Cut bread into 1-inch cubes and place in a large bowl. Drizzle oil over bread cubes until lightly covered and sprinkle with garlic powder and basil; toss to coat.

Place coated bread cubes in a grill basket in a single layer, place on grill, and cook for 10–15 minutes, or until toasted to a light golden brown; turn frequently.

Seafood Pesto Pizza
MAKES 6 SERVINGS

2 loaves	focaccia or prepared pizza crusts
4 to 6 ounces	pesto sauce
1½ cups	grated mozzarella cheese
¼ cup	grated Parmesan or Romano cheese
½ cup	ricotta cheese

Toppings:

1½ cups	peeled shrimp (sautéed in butter)
1 cup	diced crabmeat
1	large tomato, sliced
¼ cup	peeled garlic cloves
1	large sweet yellow bell pepper, sliced
5 ounces	frozen chopped spinach, thawed and drained
½	sweet onion, sliced
1 teaspoon	fresh lemon juice, to serve

Preheat grill to medium-high.

Place focaccia or pizza crusts on grill and toast 1–2 minutes, or until bread begins to brown. Remove from grill. Top toasted side with pesto sauce and half of all cheeses. Arrange shrimp, crabmeat, tomato, garlic, pepper, spinach, and onion over top. Cover with remaining cheese. Carefully return to grill. Close lid and continue grilling 2–4 minutes, or until bottom browns and cheese melts. If top is slow to melt, move to upper rack and close lid, checking every 1–2 minutes until done. If grill does not have an upper rack, place pizza on aluminum foil in grill to prevent bottom from burning while cheese melts. Sprinkle lemon juice over pizza and serve.

Grilled Bacon, Lettuce, and Tomato Sandwiches

MAKES 2 SANDWICHES

1 to 2 tablespoons	mayonnaise, or to taste
4 slices	soft white bread
8 strips	thick-cut peppered bacon, or of choice
1	large heirloom tomato, sliced salt and freshly ground pepper, to taste
2 to 4 leaves	iceberg lettuce

Preheat grill to medium low.

Spread a thin layer of mayonnaise on one side of each bread slice. Lay the bread slices on the grill grate, mayonnaise side down, and grill for 45–60 seconds, or until golden brown.

Remove from the grill and spread a layer of mayonnaise on untoasted side of bread slices; set aside.

Place the bacon on a grill mat or sheet, or a couple layers of heavy-duty aluminum foil with the edges turned up, and place that on the grill, over indirect heat. Cook and turn bacon strips every 2–3 minutes to make sure they cook evenly, until cooked as desired. Remove from the grill and let drain on paper towels.

Assemble sandwiches by arranging 4 strips of bacon on 2 slices of bread over the mayonnaise. Place 1–2 slices of tomato over the bacon, season with salt and pepper, and add lettuce. Top with remaining bread slices.

Tuna and Cheese Melts

MAKES 2 SANDWICHES

	butter, to taste
4 slices	bread, of choice
1 can (6 ounces)	tuna, drained
2 to 4 tablespoons	mayonnaise, or to taste
1 tablespoon	sweet or dill pickle relish, or to taste
2 sandwich slices	cheddar cheese
	tomato slices, optional

Preheat grill to medium high.

Lightly butter one side of each bread slice. Lay bread slices, buttered side down, on a plate.

In a small bowl, mix together the tuna, mayonnaise, and relish. Divide mixture in half and top 2 slices of bread with the tuna and the remaining slices of bread with cheese. Place filled bread slices on grill grate, buttered side down, and cook for about 2 minutes, or until lightly toasted and cheese melts. Remove from grill and place a couple of tomato slices over tuna mixture on each sandwich, if using. Top with remaining bread slices.

Variation: Try one of our family favorites and replace the tuna mixture with raspberry jam.

Quesadilla Stacks

MAKES 4 SERVINGS

8 (8-inch)	**flour tortillas**
	vegetable oil or softened butter
4 cups	**grated Monterey Jack or cheddar cheese**
	favorite toppings such as: sliced grilled chicken, green onions, fresh spinach leaves, black olives, green chiles, tomatoes, jalapeños, or avocado
	favorite salsa, to serve

Preheat grill to medium high.

Brush both sides of each tortilla with oil. Place tortillas on grill for 1–3 minutes, or until golden brown underneath. Flip tortillas over and sprinkle evenly with cheese. Layer your choice of toppings over 4 of the tortillas and continue to cook until cheese melts and the bottoms turn golden; remove from grill. Place 1 of the cheese-only tortillas over the top of each filled tortilla, cheese side down. Serve with salsa on the side.

#26-48

BEEF

Classic Rib-Eye

MAKES 2–4 SERVINGS

2 to 4   **rib-eye steaks**
1 recipe   **Steve's Famous Dry Rub (page 119)**
         smoker pouch (see page 10)

Evenly rub the entire surface of each steak with Steve's Famous Dry Rub. If time allows, let the steaks rest at room temperature for 20–30 minutes before grilling.

Place a smoker pouch directly on the fire, under the grill grate, and turn grill to high heat until smoke begins to rise from the holes.

Place steaks on grill grate directly over the heat and sear for 1 minute on each side. Turn grill down to medium-low heat halfway through searing the second side. Move the steaks to area of indirect heat, the cooler side of the grill, and cook to desired doneness, turning the steaks once halfway through grilling process.

Remove from grill when the internal temperature of the steaks read approximately 5 degrees lower than the desired finished cooking temperature. Place on a serving plate and allow steaks to rest for about 5 minutes before serving.

Tempting T-Bone

MAKES 2–4 SERVINGS

2 to 4 (1-inch-thick)	T-bone steaks
1 to 2 tablespoons	Steve's Famous Dry Rub (page 119), or to taste
1 to 2 tablespoons	garlic salt, or to taste smoker pouch (see page 10)

Evenly rub one side of each steak with the dry rub and the other side with garlic salt. Place steaks on a large plate and let sit at room temperature for 20–30 minutes before grilling, if possible.

Preheat grill to high.

Place the smoker pouch directly on the fire, under the grate, until smoke begins to rise from holes. Place steaks on grill grate directly over high heat for 30 seconds, then turn and sear the other side for another 30 seconds, turning the heat down to medium halfway through searing the second side.

Move the steaks to the cooler side of the grill away from direct heat and cook to desired doneness, turning the steaks once about halfway through grilling. Remove from grill when the internal temperature on an instant-read thermometer reaches approximately 5 degrees lower than the desired finished temperature. Allow steaks to rest for about 5 minutes before serving.

Honey-Garlic BBQ Sirloin

MAKES 2–4 SERVINGS

2 to 4 (1½-inch thick)	**sirloin steaks**
1 recipe	**Honey-Garlic BBQ Sauce (page 124)**

Preheat grill to high.

Place steaks on grill grate directly over high heat for 30 seconds, then turn and sear the other side for another 30 seconds, turning the heat down to medium halfway through searing the second side. Move the steaks to the cooler side of the grill away from direct heat and cook to desired doneness, turning the steaks once about halfway through grilling.

As the steaks begin to reach optimal temperature, brush the tops with sauce and continue to grill for about 1–1½ minutes until the sauce starts to glaze over. Turn the steaks over and brush with sauce, repeating the process.

Remove from grill when the internal temperature on an instant-read thermometer reaches approximately 5 degrees lower than the desired finished temperature. Allow steaks to rest for about 5 minutes before serving.

Smoky Mop Sauce Steaks

MAKES 2–4 SERVINGS

	smoker pouch (see page 10)
2 to 4	beef steaks, any variety
	Mop Sauce (page 122)
	barbecue sauce, of choice
	salt and pepper, to taste

Place smoker pouch directly on the fire under the grate and turn to high heat until smoke begins to rise from holes. Turn grill down to medium-low heat.

Place steaks on upper rack or use foil under steaks if grill only has one level or cooks hot. Turn steaks every 5–6 minutes, coating with Mop Sauce each time, until desired doneness (see Advanced Grilling Tips, page 12). Season with salt and pepper.

Remove steaks from grill and allow to rest 2–3 minutes before serving. Serve with barbecue sauce for dipping.

Island-Style Sirloin Strips

MAKES 2–4 SERVINGS

1½ pounds	sirloin tip steak, cut into ½-inch-thick strips
1½ to 2 cups	Island-Style Marinade (page 124)
	hot cooked rice, to serve

Place steak strips and marinade in a large covered bowl or ziplock bag, stir or shake to coat, and marinate in the refrigerator overnight.

When ready to cook, preheat grill to high.

Remove sirloin strips from marinade and lay across grill grate; cook for about 30 seconds on each side. Turn heat down to medium and continue cooking for 8–12 minutes, or until desired doneness, turning frequently. Serve over hot cooked rice.

Boil the leftover marinade in a saucepan over high heat to make it safe to use as a warmed sauce drizzled over the rice.

Jazzed-Up BBQ Steak
MAKES 2–4 SERVINGS

> **2 to 4** **sirloin steaks**
> **1 recipe** **Jazzed-Up BBQ Sauce (page 120)**

Preheat grill to high.

Place steaks on grill grate directly over the heat and sear for 1 minute on each side. Turn grill down to medium low halfway through searing the second side. Move the steaks to area of indirect heat, the cooler side of the grill, and cook to desired doneness, turning the steaks once halfway through grilling process.

As steaks begin to reach optimal internal temperature, brush the tops with sauce and continue to cook for 60–90 seconds, until sauce starts to glaze over. Turn the steaks and brush the other side with the sauce allowing same amount of time to glaze.

Remove from grill when the internal temperature of the steaks read approximately 5 degrees lower than the desired finished cooking temperature. Place on a serving plate and allow steaks to rest for about 5 minutes before serving.

Teriyaki Steak

MAKES 2–4 SERVINGS

1 cup	Kikkoman soy sauce
1 cup	sugar
1 clove	garlic, peeled and minced
1 tablespoon	grated fresh ginger
3	green onions, sliced
2 to 4	steaks of choice, such as cube steak

Combine all ingredients except steaks in a medium saucepan and heat, stirring constantly, until sugar dissolves. Pour into a deep dish to cool for a few minutes and add the steaks, turning to coat. Let steaks marinate for 1–2 hours, and no longer, before grilling. Remove steaks from refrigerator and marinade, place on a plate, and bring to room temperature.

Preheat grill to medium low.

Place steaks on grill grate and cook, turning every 4–5 minutes, until desired doneness. Remove steaks from grill and allow to rest for about 5 minutes before serving.

Garlic-Rubbed Steaks

MAKES 2–4 SERVINGS

2 to 4 (1–1½-inch-thick) **steaks of choice, such as porterhouse, T-bone, rib-eye, New York strip, or top sirloin**
1 tablespoon **minced fresh garlic, or to taste**
2 tablespoons **food-safe rock salt**
Montreal Steak Seasoning, to taste

Preheat grill to high.

Rub both sides of each steak evenly with minced garlic and rock salt. Place steaks on grill grate over direct heat and sear for 1 minute on each side. Turn heat down to medium and cook to desired doneness. Sprinkle both sides of each steak with steak seasoning, remove from grill, and allow to rest for about 5 minutes before serving.

Peppered Sirloin Steaks Smothered in Cream Sauce

MAKES 2–4 SERVINGS

Sauce:

½	sweet onion, sliced
1 teaspoon	minced garlic
1 tablespoon	butter
1 teaspoon	water
1 teaspoon	white grape juice
1 teaspoon	apple juice or cider
½ pint	whipping cream or half-and-half
	salt, to taste
1 tablespoon	coarsely ground pepper
2 to 4	sirloin steaks

Sauté onion and garlic in butter in a large frying pan 5 minutes, or until tender. Add remaining sauce ingredients and bring to a boil, stirring constantly. Season with salt and simmer until ready to serve over steaks.

Press pepper into steaks and grill to desired doneness (see Advanced Grilling Tips, page 12). Serve with warm cream sauce.

Korean Ribs
MAKES 2-4 SERVINGS

3/4 cup	water
3/4 cup	soy sauce
1/2 cup	brown sugar, firmly packed
1/2 cup	rice or cider vinegar
1 tablespoon	ketchup
1 teaspoon	fresh grated or minced ginger
2 teaspoons	minced garlic
2 tablespoons	sesame oil (optional)
1 pound	beef ribs, about 1/4 inch thick
3 tablespoons	green onions, finely chopped

Mix together water, soy sauce, brown sugar, vinegar, ketchup, ginger, garlic, and sesame oil. Marinate meat in mixture 24 hours or overnight, stirring occasionally.

Preheat grill to medium low.

Turn grill down to low heat. Grill ribs slowly for 15-20 minutes, or until done, turning frequently. Garnish with green onions.

Variation: For a spicier version, add 1 teaspoon red pepper flakes and/or 1/2 teaspoon cayenne pepper.

Steakhouse Special

MAKES 2–4 SERVINGS

2 to 4	steaks, any variety
1 cup	nonalcoholic beer
2 teaspoons	brown sugar
1/2 teaspoon	seasoned salt
1/4 teaspoon	freshly ground pepper

Place steaks in a shallow pan and pour beer over top. Marinate 1 hour in the refrigerator.

Remove steaks from marinade. Mix together dry ingredients and rub on both sides of steaks. Let sit with dry rub 30 minutes. Preheat grill to high. Place steaks on grill 1 minute per side, then turn grill down to medium heat. Grill 10–15 minutes, or until desired doneness, turning frequently.

#37

Sweet and Spicy Dry Rub Ribs

MAKES 3–5 SERVINGS

	Steve's Famous Dry Rub (page 119)
4 to 8	country-style beef ribs
1 1/2 cups	salsa, divided

Rub dry rub into ribs and let sit about 1 hour before grilling. Preheat grill to medium. Lightly oil the grate.

Grill 15–20 minutes, or to desired doneness, turning frequently. Just before taking ribs off the grill, brush with 1/2 cup of the salsa. Serve ribs with remaining salsa over top.

Patrick's Pepper Steak

MAKES 2–4 SERVINGS

	coarsely crushed peppercorns, to taste
2 to 4	sirloin steaks
	salt and pepper, to taste

Sprinkle peppercorns on both sides of steaks, pressing into steaks well. Allow them to sit at room temperature 20 minutes before grilling. Sear steaks over direct high heat 1 minute per side, then turn grill down to medium heat and cook until desired doneness (see Advanced Grilling Tips, page 12). Season with salt and pepper. Remove steaks from grill and allow to rest 2–3 minutes before serving.

Roberto's South American Lime Ribs

MAKES 3–5 SERVINGS

4 to 8	boneless beef ribs
3/4 cup	rock salt
2 tablespoons	minced garlic
8	limes, sectioned

Preheat grill to medium. Coat ribs liberally with salt and press in. Sprinkle with garlic. Lightly oil the grill. Grill 15–20 minutes, or to desired doneness, turning frequently. Remove from grill and squeeze limes over top for a great flavor.

Smoked Honey-Garlic BBQ Ribs

MAKES 3–5 SERVINGS

3 to 4 pounds	**beef or pork ribs** **Honey-Garlic BBQ Sauce** **(page 124)** **smoker pouch (see page 10)**

Marinate ribs 30 minutes or overnight in sauce.

Place smoker pouch directly on the fire under the grate and turn to high heat until smoke begins to rise from holes. Sear ribs over direct high heat 1 minute per side. Turn grill down to medium heat.

Grill 15–25 minutes, or to desired doneness, turning frequently. Baste during last 5 minutes of grilling with leftover marinade that has been boiled.

Hunter's West Coast BBQ Ribs

MAKES 4–6 SERVINGS

½ can	regular (not diet) cola
½ cup	Italian salad dressing
1 tablespoon	liquid smoke
3 to 4 pounds	country-style beef ribs
1 bottle	barbecue sauce, of choice

Mix cola, Italian dressing, and liquid smoke together in a large bowl. Add meat to the bowl, cover, and marinate overnight.

Grill ribs over medium heat, turning frequently, and coating with barbecue sauce during last 5 minutes of total cook time (see Advanced Grilling Tips, page 12).

Variation: For extra-tender ribs, boil them in water for 1 hour before marinating.

Steak Kebabs with Bite
MAKES 2–4 SERVINGS

2 to 4	country-style beef ribs or steaks, cut into 1-inch cubes
½ cup	cider vinegar
1 cup	vegetable oil
1 envelope (1 ounce)	onion soup mix
2 teaspoons	Mr. Yoshida's Gourmet Sauce or teriyaki or soy sauce, of choice
2 tablespoons	minced fresh garlic
2 to 4 (10–12-inch)	metal or bamboo* skewers

Place the meat in a medium bowl. In a separate bowl, mix together the vinegar, oil, soup mix, sauce, and garlic until well combined. Pour over the meat and stir to coat. Marinate, covered, in refrigerator for 2–3 hours.

Preheat grill to medium high.

Thread marinated meat on skewers and lay across grill grate. Cook, turning every 5 minutes, until desired doneness.

Variation: Alternate whole mushrooms, bell pepper wedges, and onion wedges between steak pieces before grilling.

*If you use wooden skewers, soak them in water for 30 minutes prior to use to prevent burning.

Perfect Prime Rib Roast

MAKES 4 SERVINGS

1 (2-rib)	**prime rib roast, about 4 pounds**
2 tablespoons	**olive oil**
½ cup	**food-safe rock salt (It is okay to use table salt, just be a little more conservative.)**
3 tablespoons	**garlic salt**

Lightly coat the roast and ribs evenly with oil and rub in the rock salt and garlic salt.

Preheat grill to medium high.

Place the roast on the upper rack of grill, if possible, or in a cooler section of the grill out of direct heat. Position a large dripping pan under roast on lower rack or under the grill grate. Close lid and cook for 20–30 minutes per pound; turning roast every 45 minutes. Remove roast from grill when internal temperature gets within 5–10 degrees of desired level of doneness. Internal temperature of roast will rise another 10 degrees after you remove it from the grill. Shoot for an internal temperature of 130 degrees, if you like it rare, and 150 degrees if you like a medium cook. If you want it well-done, leave the roast on the grill until it reaches an internal temperature of 165 degrees.

Remove roast from grill to a serving platter, tent loosely with aluminum foil, and let it rest for 15 minutes.

#44

Basic Brisket

MAKES 3–5 SERVINGS

1	beef brisket
	Steve's Famous Dry Rub (page 119)
½ cup	salsa
¼ cup	chili sauce
3 tablespoons	orange marmalade
	salt and pepper, to taste

Preheat grill to high.

Seal the juices in brisket by searing it on grill 1–2 minutes per side. Turn grill down to low heat and grill brisket slowly, 20–30 minutes per pound of meat. Turn frequently until done.

Combine salsa, chili sauce, and orange marmalade, and use as a baste for the brisket during the last 5 minutes of grilling. When brisket is done, season with salt and pepper.

Shredded Beef Brisket

MAKES 6–8 SERVINGS

	smoker pouch (see page 10)
1 (3- to 4-pound)	beef brisket
1 recipe	Mop Sauce (page 122)
2 cups	favorite barbecue sauce, warmed
6 to 8	hamburger buns, toasted
	prepared coleslaw, to serve

Preheat grill to high.

Place smoker pouch directly on the fire under the grate and turn grill to high heat until smoke begins to rise from the holes. Immediately turn heat to medium low and place brisket on upper rack of grill, if possible. If there is no upper rack, place brisket on a large piece of heavy-duty aluminum foil. Close lid and cook for 30 minutes before basting with Mop Sauce. Continue to cook, turning and basting the brisket every 30 minutes until internal temperature reaches 165–180 degrees, not to exceed 190 degrees. Remove from grill to a serving platter, tent loosely with aluminum foil, and let it rest for 10–15 minutes.

Using two forks, shred meat into fine pieces and mix in warmed barbecue sauce, or serve it on the side. Serve shredded meat on toasted buns topped with coleslaw.

Andie's BBQ Burgers

MAKES 4–5 SERVINGS

1 pound	lean ground beef
½ envelope (½ ounce)	dry onion soup mix
¼ cup	ketchup
2 tablespoons	brown sugar
1 teaspoon	vinegar
1 teaspoon	dry mustard
	salt and pepper, to taste
4 or 5 slices	cheese
4 or 5	hamburger buns

Preheat grill to medium.

Thoroughly mix together the ground beef, soup mix, ketchup, brown sugar, vinegar, mustard, and salt and pepper by hand. Form ground beef mixture into four or five hamburger patties; remember, they will shrink when cooked.

Grill 10–20 minutes, or until desired doneness, turning every 4–5 minutes. Add cheese to the burgers, then remove from heat. Serve on hamburger buns.

Juiciest BBQ Hamburgers Ever

MAKES 4–5 SERVINGS

1 pound	lean ground beef
¼ cup	barbecue sauce
2 tablespoons	Worcestershire sauce
¼	onion, finely chopped
¼ cup	instant oats
4 or 5 slices	cheese
4 or 5	hamburger buns

Preheat grill to medium.

Thoroughly mix together the ground beef, barbecue sauce, Worcestershire sauce, onion, and oats by hand. Form ground beef mixture into four or five hamburger patties; remember, they will shrink when cooked.

Grill 10–20 minutes, or until desired doneness, turning every 4–5 minutes. Add cheese to the burgers and remove from heat. Serve on hamburger buns.

Steve's Dry Rub Burgers

MAKES 2–4 SERVINGS

1 pound	lean ground beef*
	Steve's Famous Dry Rub (page 119)
4 or 5	cheese slices
4 or 5	hamburger buns

Preheat grill to medium.

Form ground beef into four or five hamburger patties; remember they will shrink when cooked. Sprinkle with dry rub and grill 10–20 minutes, or until desired doneness, turning every 4–5 minutes. Add cheese to the burgers and remove from heat. Serve on hamburger buns.

*For a time-saver, try using premade or frozen hamburger patties.

POULTRY

Simplest BBQ Chicken

MAKES 4–6 SERVINGS

4 to 6 **boneless, skinless chicken breasts**
thyme or tarragon
barbecue sauce, of choice
salt and pepper, to taste

Preheat grill to medium low.

Place chicken over grill grate and cook, turning every 4–5 minutes, until juices run clear and internal temperature reaches 165 degrees. Sprinkle a light coating of thyme or tarragon over chicken. Baste with barbecue sauce during the last 5 minutes of grilling, turning every 1–2 minutes.

Season with salt and pepper. Serve chicken as desired. Great on Caesar salads.

Variation: Use a whole chicken that has been cut and quartered. Grill for 30–40 minutes, or until internal temperature reaches 165 degrees. Follow directions above for basting. This variation can be used for most of the chicken recipes in this chapter.

Jazzed-Up Chicken

MAKES 4–6 SERVINGS

4 to 6	**boneless, skinless chicken breasts**
1 recipe	**Jazzed-Up BBQ Sauce (page 120)**
2	**red bell peppers, sliced**
1	**yellow onion, peeled and sliced**
1 tablespoon	**butter**

Preheat grill to medium low.

Place chicken over grill grate and cook, turning every 4–5 minutes, until juices run clear and internal temperature reaches 165 degrees.

Baste chicken with sauce during last 5 minutes of cooking, turning every 1–2 minutes. Remove chicken from grill and let rest for 2–3 minutes before serving.

While chicken is cooking, place the peppers, onion, and butter in a medium frying pan, and sauté until tender. Serve over chicken.

Steve's Famous Dry Rub Chicken on a Can

MAKES 4–5 SERVINGS

	smoker pouch (see page 10)
2 tablespoons	butter, softened
1 recipe	Steve's Famous Dry Rub (page 119)
1	whole chicken, rinsed and patted dry
1 can (12 ounces)	regular soda such as a cola or Dr. Pepper

Place smoker pouch directly on the fire under the grill grate and turn grill to high heat until smoke begins to rise from the holes. Reduce heat to medium low.

Rub butter evenly over the chicken, then rub the dry mix over the chicken to cover. Let sit at room temperature for at least 30 minutes before grilling.

Remove the upper grill rack and check to see if the whole chicken will fit standing up in the grill with the lid down. After you thoroughly wash and dry the outside of the soda can, check to make sure the can will fit easily into the chicken's cavity. Remove the chicken and open the can of soda, placing the can on the grill rack or grate. Lower the chicken onto the can so that if fits into the cavity. Pull the legs forward to form a tripod to help give it some balance.

If your grill cooks hot, place a sheet of heavy-duty aluminum foil underneath the chicken. Close the lid and let it cook for 20 minutes per pound, or until an instant-read thermometer inserted into the thickest part of the thigh reaches 180 degrees (make sure not to touch bone).

Carefully transfer the chicken and can to a cutting board; both will be extremely hot. Let rest for 10–15 minutes, remove the can from the chicken and carve to serve.

#52
Smoked Honey-Garlic Chicken
MAKES 4–6 SERVINGS

4 to 6	boneless, skinless chicken breasts
1 recipe	Honey-Garlic BBQ Sauce (page 124)
	smoker pouch (see page 10)
	cinnamon, to serve

Place chicken in a large ziplock bag. Add sauce, toss or shake to coat, and place in refrigerator to marinate for at least 30 minutes, or overnight, before grilling.

When ready to grill the chicken, place smoker pouch directly on the fire under the grill grate and turn the grill to high heat until smoke begins to rise from holes. Reduce heat to low, place chicken over grill grate, and cook, turning every 4–5 minutes, until juices run clear and internal temperature reaches 165 degrees.

Dust chicken with cinnamon when ready to serve.

Smoky Mopped Chicken

MAKES 4–6 SERVINGS

	smoker pouch (see page 10)
4 to 6	**boneless, skinless chicken breasts**
	Mop Sauce (page 122)
	barbecue sauce, of choice

Place smoker pouch directly on the fire under the grate and turn to high heat until smoke begins to rise from holes. Immediately turn grill down to low heat.

Place chicken on upper grill rack, or on aluminum foil if grill only has one level or cooks hot. Turn chicken every 4–5 minutes, coating with Mop Sauce each time, until juices run clear and internal temperature reaches 165 degrees. Serve with barbecue sauce.

Grandma's Cola Chicken

MAKES 3–5 SERVINGS

1 cup	**flour**
1½ pounds	**chicken tenders**
1 bottle (14 ounces)	**ketchup**
½ can (12 ounces)	**regular cola**

Preheat grill to low.

Place flour in a medium bowl. Working in batches, dredge chicken tenders through flour to coat.

In a separate bowl, stir together the ketchup and cola until thoroughly combined; set aside.

Place chicken over grill grate and cook, turning every 4–5 minutes, until juices run clear and internal temperature reaches 165 degrees.

Baste chicken with cola sauce during the last 5 minutes of grilling, turning every 1–2 minutes.

Tangy Chicken
MAKES 4–6 SERVINGS

4 to 6	**boneless, skinless chicken breasts**
1 cup	**cider vinegar**
½ cup	**vegetable oil**
3 teaspoons	**minced fresh garlic**
½ teaspoon	**poultry seasoning**
1 tablespoon	**coarse salt**

Place chicken in a large ziplock bag. In a small bowl, mix together the remaining ingredients, reserving some of the marinade to baste chicken with during the last few minutes of cooking time. Pour marinade over chicken and toss or shake to coat. Close bag and place in refrigerator to marinate overnight.

Preheat grill to low.

Place chicken over grill grate and cook, turning every 4–5 minutes, until juices run clear and internal temperature reaches 165 degrees.

Once the chicken is done, baste with reserved marinade, and leave on grill long enough for the marinade to glaze over a bit.

Island-Grilled Teriyaki Chicken

MAKES 2–5 SERVINGS

8 to 10	**boneless, skinless chicken thighs**
2 cups	**Mr. Yoshida's Gourmet Sauce or teriyaki sauce, of choice**
1 tablespoon	**minced fresh garlic, or to taste**
½	**medium sweet onion, peeled and finely chopped**
2	**green onions, chopped**

Place chicken in a large ziplock bag. In a medium bowl, mix together the remaining ingredients, reserving some of the marinade to baste chicken with during the last few minutes of cooking time. Pour over chicken and toss or shake to coat. Close bag and place in refrigerator to marinate overnight.

Preheat grill to low.

Place chicken over grill grate and cook, turning every 4–5 minutes, until juices run clear and internal temperature reaches 165 degrees.

Once the chicken is done, baste with reserved marinade and leave on grill long enough for the marinade to glaze over.

Succulent Chicken

MAKES 3–5 SERVINGS

8 to 10	boneless, skinless chicken thighs
1 cup	soy sauce
1 cup	water
2 cups	brown sugar
1 tablespoon	minced fresh garlic
1 tablespoon	minced fresh ginger
2	lemon or orange slices
2 tablespoons	minced fresh green onion

Place chicken in a large ziplock bag. In a medium bowl, mix together the remaining ingredients and pour over the chicken; toss or shake to coat. Close bag and place in refrigerator to marinate overnight.

Preheat grill to low.

Place chicken over grill grate and cook, turning every 4–5 minutes, until juices run clear and internal temperature reaches 165 degrees.

Grilled Chili Sauce Chicken

MAKES 4 SERVINGS

1½ cups	chili sauce
¾ cup	red-wine vinegar
1 tablespoon	horseradish
2 tablespoons	minced garlic
½ teaspoon	salt
4	boneless, skinless chicken breasts

Mix all ingredients together except chicken in a large bowl. Reserve half of marinade. Add chicken to bowl and marinate 30 minutes.

Preheat grill to medium low.

Place chicken over grill grate and cook, turning every 4–5 minutes, until juices run clear and internal temperature reaches 165 degrees. During last 5 minutes of grilling, coat with reserved marinade.

Heat any remaining marinade in a small saucepan until it comes to a full boil, stirring occasionally. Serve with chicken.

#59

Jen's Egyptian Grilled Chicken

MAKES 4 SERVINGS

4	boneless, skinless chicken breasts
1 cup	plain yogurt
3 tablespoons	fresh lemon juice
3 teaspoons	minced garlic
1 teaspoon	salt
½ teaspoon	cinnamon
½ teaspoon	pepper
¼ teaspoon	ground cloves
¼ teaspoon	ground cardamom*

Place chicken in a large ziplock bag or covered bowl. In a medium bowl, mix together the remaining ingredients; combine with the chicken. Cover and place in refrigerator to marinate overnight.

Preheat grill to low.

Place chicken over grill grate and cook, turning every 4–5 minutes, until juices run clear and internal temperature reaches 165 degrees.

*This expensive spice adds a lot of flavor, but it can be left out. Try finding a grocer that sells spices by the bulk and only purchase what you need.

Orange-Sesame Chicken

MAKES 8 SERVINGS

8	boneless, skinless chicken thighs
½ cup	orange juice
1 tablespoon	lemon juice
1 tablespoon	vinegar
2 teaspoons	yellow mustard
2 tablespoons	toasted sesame oil

Place chicken in a shallow baking dish or a large ziplock bag. In a small bowl, mix together the orange juice, lemon juice, vinegar, and mustard. Whisk the oil in slowly. Pour marinade over chicken, reserving some of the marinade to baste chicken with during the last few minutes of cooking time. Pour over chicken and toss or shake to coat. Cover and place in refrigerator to marinate for 2 hours.

Preheat grill to medium low.

Place chicken over grill grate and cook, turning every 4–5 minutes, until juices run clear and internal temperature reaches 165 degrees.

Once the chicken is done, baste with reserved marinade, and leave on grill long enough for the marinade to glaze over a bit.

Italian Chicken

MAKES 3–5 SERVINGS

1 bottle	Italian salad dressing
1/2 teaspoon	salt
1/4 teaspoon	pepper
1/2 cup	salsa
1 teaspoon	Worcestershire sauce
1/4 to 1/2 cup	diced sweet onion
1 teaspoon	minced garlic
1/2 to 1 cup	orange juice
1 1/2 pounds	boneless, skinless chicken tenders

With a wire whisk, mix all ingredients together except chicken in a bowl. Reserve half of marinade. Add chicken to bowl and marinate, covered, at least 30 minutes or overnight.

Preheat grill to medium low.

Place chicken over grill grate and cook, turning every 4–5 minutes, until juices run clear and internal temperature reaches 165 degrees. During last 5 minutes of grilling, coat with reserved marinade.

Monday-Night-Special Buffalo Wings

MAKES 2–4 SERVINGS

1 cup	spicy barbecue sauce, of choice
2 to 3 tablespoons	Tabasco Pepper Sauce, or to taste
2 tablespoons	brown sugar
1 tablespoon	vinegar
1/4 teaspoon	freshly ground pepper
2 dozen	chicken wings or wing drummies
	celery sticks, to serve
	blue cheese salad dressing, to serve

In a small saucepan, combine sauces, brown sugar, vinegar, and pepper and bring to a boil. Remove from heat, pour into a large bowl, and let cool for 15 minutes. Add chicken wings to marinade and chill 2 hours or more.

Preheat grill to medium low.

Place wings over grill grate and cook for 10–15 minutes, or until juices run clear and internal temperature reaches 165 degrees, turning every 4–5 minutes.

Serve with celery and salad dressing on the side.

Stuffed Chicken Breast

MAKES 6–8 SERVINGS

½	sweet onion, sliced
1 tablespoon	minced garlic
2 tablespoons	butter
8 (6–8 ounce)	boneless, skinless chicken breasts
	flour
	salt and pepper, to taste

Preheat grill to medium low.

Sauté onion and garlic in butter. Cut a pocket in the side of each chicken breast and stuff with onion mixture. Roll each breast in flour.

Place chicken over grill grate and cook, turning every 4–5 minutes, until juices run clear and internal temperature reaches 165 degrees. Season with salt and pepper.

Crabby Stuffed Chicken Breast

MAKES 8 SERVINGS

Stuffing:

1 can (6 ounces)	**crabmeat**
1 package (8 ounces)	**cream cheese, softened**
1 tablespoon	**minced garlic**
¼ cup	**grated Parmesan cheese**
8 (6–8 ounce)	**boneless, skinless chicken breasts** **flour** **salt and pepper, to taste**

Preheat grill to medium low.

Combine stuffing ingredients. Cut a pocket in the side of each chicken breast and fill with a heaping tablespoon of stuffing. Roll each breast in flour.

Place chicken over grill grate and cook, turning every 4–5 minutes, until juices run clear and internal temperature reaches 165 degrees. Season with salt and pepper.

Tapasa's Samoan-Style Chicken

MAKES 3–5 SERVINGS

> **8 to 10** **boneless, skinless chicken thighs**
> **Island-Style Marinade (page 124)**

Marinate chicken in sauce in a covered large bowl or ziplock plastic bag overnight.

Preheat grill to low.

Place chicken over grill grate and cook, turning every 4–5 minutes, until juices run clear and internal temperature reaches 165 degrees.

#66

Alabama-Style BBQ Chicken

MAKES 4–6 SERVINGS

> **4 to 6** **boneless, skinless chicken breasts**
> **1 recipe** **Alabama White BBQ**
> **Sauce (page 121)**

Preheat grill to low.

Place chicken over grill grate and cook, turning every 4–5 minutes, until juices run clear and internal temperature reaches 165 degrees.

During the last 5 minutes of cooking, coat the chicken with sauce, cook for about 2 minutes, and turn to baste the other side, cooking for 2–3 minutes more.

Bacon-Stuffed Chicken Breast

MAKES 8 SERVINGS

8 (6–8 ounce)	boneless, skinless chicken breasts
8	slices bacon, cooked
	flour
	salt and pepper, to taste

Preheat grill to medium low.

Cut a pocket in the side of each chicken breast and stuff with a slice of cooked bacon. Roll each breast in flour and then place on grill. Turn chicken every 4–5 minutes until juices run clear and internal temperature reaches 165 degrees. Season with salt and pepper.

Jazzy BBQ Turkey Legs

MAKES 2–4 SERVINGS

2 to 4	turkey legs
1 recipe	Jazzed-Up BBQ Sauce (page 120)

Preheat grill to medium high.

Place turkey legs over grill grate and cook for 30–45 minutes, or until juices run clear and internal temperature reaches 165 degrees, turning occasionally.

During the last 5 minutes of cooking, baste turkey with sauce, turning to coat completely. Serve hot with any extra sauce, heated, on the side.

Smoked Honey-Garlic BBQ Turkey

MAKES 2–4 SERVINGS

2 to 4	**turkey breasts**
	Honey-Garlic BBQ Sauce (page 124)
	smoker pouch (see page 10)
2	**green bell peppers, sliced**
	olive oil

Add turkey to sauce and marinate at least 30 minutes or overnight.

Place smoker pouch directly on the fire under the grate and turn to high heat until smoke begins to rise from holes. Immediately turn down to medium-low heat.

Place turkey on upper rack for best smoking. Cook turkey 20–30 minutes, turning frequently, until juices run clear and internal temperature reaches 165 degrees.

In a frying pan, sauté peppers in butter until tender and serve over turkey.

#70-82

PORK

Crazy-Good Brined Pork Chops

MAKES 2–4 SERVINGS

2 to 4 (1-inch-thick)	**center-cut pork chops or steaks**
1 recipe	**Pork and Poultry Brine (page 125)**
1 recipe	**Steve's Brown Sugar Rub (page 118)**

Place chops in brine and marinate in refrigerator for 45–60 minutes prior to grilling. Make sure there is enough brine to completely cover the chops.

Remove chops from brine, rinse, and pat dry.

Preheat grill to medium.

Season both sides of each chop with the dry rub, and then place in coolest part of the grill, out of direct heat. Close lid and cook for 10–12 minutes per side, or until internal temperature reaches 145–160 degrees, depending on your taste. Remove chops from grill and let rest for about 10 minutes before serving.

Jazzed-Up BBQ Pork Steaks

MAKES 2–4 SERVINGS

2 to 4 (1-inch thick) **center-cut pork chops or steaks**
Jazzed-Up BBQ Sauce
(page 120), divided
cayenne pepper

Marinate pork in half of sauce at least 30 minutes before grilling. Set remaining sauce aside.

Preheat grill to medium.

Grill 15–20 minutes, or until internal temperature reaches 145–160 degrees, depending on your taste.

Add a pinch of cayenne to reserved sauce. During last 5 minutes of cooking, coat chops or steaks with reserved sauce; turn every 1–2 minutes. Remove pork from grill and allow to rest 2–3 minutes before serving.

Big Red's Chops

MAKES 2–4 SERVINGS

2 to 4 (1-inch-thick)	**center-cut pork chops or steaks**
1 recipe	**Big Red's Spicy Dry Rub (page 119)**
1 cup	**barbecue sauce, of choice, to serve**

Rub chops thoroughly with dry rub and let sit 20–40 minutes before grilling.

Preheat grill to medium.

Place chops on grill grate out of direct heat. Cook for 10–12 minutes per side, or until internal temperature reaches 145–160 degrees, depending on taste. Serve with barbecue sauce on the side.

Variation: Try Steve's Famous Dry Rub (page 119) in place of Big Red's Spicy Dry Rub.

Smoked Honey-Garlic BBQ Pork

MAKES 2–4 SERVINGS

1 recipe	**Honey-Garlic BBQ Sauce (page 124)**
¼ teaspoon	**curry powder**
2 to 4 (1-inch-thick)	**center-cut pork chops or steaks**
	smoker pouch (see page 10)

In a small bowl, combine Honey-Garlic BBQ Sauce with curry powder; reserve some of the sauce for basting.

Place chops in a shallow dish and cover with the marinade. Let rest at room temperature for 30–60 minutes before grilling.

Place smoker pouch directly on the fire under the grate and turn grill to high heat until smoke begins to rise from holes. Immediately turn heat down to medium low.

Place chops on grill grate and cook for 15–20 minutes on the upper rack for best smoking results. Chops are done when the internal temperature reaches 145–160 degrees. During the last 5 minutes of cooking, baste chops with reserved sauce, turning every 2 minutes. Remove from grill and allow to rest for 2–3 minutes before serving.

Smoked & Mopped Pulled Pork

MAKES 4–6 SERVINGS

	smoker pouch (see page 10)
1 (3- to 5-pound)	pork shoulder roast
	Mop Sauce (page 122)
2 cups	barbecue sauce, of choice
4 to 6	sandwich buns, toasted
	coleslaw, to serve

Place smoker pouch directly on the fire under the grate and turn to high heat until smoke begins to rise from holes. Immediately turn down to medium heat.

Place roast on upper grill rack, or use foil under roast if grill only has one level. Begin basting roast after 30 minutes of grilling, and repeat this process every 30 minutes, until done. Grill until the internal temperature reaches 165–180 degrees, turning every 15–20 minutes. Remove from grill and allow to rest 10–15 minutes.

Using two forks, tear meat into fine shreds. Mix shredded meat with heated barbecue sauce, or serve separately. Serve on toasted buns with coleslaw on the side or on the sandwich.

Raspberry Pork Loin

MAKES 4–6 SERVINGS

2 (1-pound)	pork tenderloins
1 recipe	Pork and Poultry Brine (page 125) or more if needed
1 recipe	Steve's Brown Sugar Rub (page 118), to taste

Raspberry BBQ Sauce:

1 cup	fresh raspberry jam with seeds
1 bottle (18 ounces)	barbecue sauce, of choice
	finely diced onion, brown sugar, mustard, or horseradish, to taste, optional

Place tenderloins in a deep dish and cover with brine. Marinate for 60 minutes per pound before grilling. Remove from brine, rinse well, and pat dry. Evenly coat tenderloins with rub.

Preheat grill to medium.

Place tenderloins on grill grate and cook for 30–40 minutes per side, or until internal temperature reaches 145–165 degrees. As you reach desired temperature, reduce heat to low. Mix together the ingredients for the Raspberry BBQ Sauce and baste tenderloins during the last 3–4 minutes of cooking time until glazed. Turn and baste the other side of each loin, allowing sauce to glaze over, about 1 minute.

Cilantro Pork Steak
MAKES 2 SERVINGS

2 **pork steaks or pork chops**
1 cup **chopped fresh cilantro leaves**
salt and pepper, to taste
garlic salt, to taste

Preheat grill to medium low.

Sprinkle pork with some of the cilantro leaves and grill 20 minutes or until internal temperature reaches 145–160 degrees, turning every 4–5 minutes, coating with cilantro leaves each time. Season with salt, pepper, and garlic salt.

Sweet-as-Honey Pork Loin

MAKES 4–6 SERVINGS

2 (1-pound)	pork tenderloins
1 recipe	Pork and Poultry Brine (page 125) or more if needed
1 recipe	Steve's Brown Sugar Rub (page 118)
	honey, to taste

Place tenderloins in a deep dish and cover with brine. Marinate for 60 minutes per pound before grilling. Remove from brine, rinse well, and pat dry. Evenly coat tenderloins with rub.

Preheat grill to medium.

Place tenderloins on grill grate and cook for 30–40 minutes per side, or until internal temperature reaches 145–165 degrees. As you reach desired temperature, drizzle honey evenly over the tenderloins during the last 3–4 minutes of cooking time until glazed. Turn and drizzle honey on the other side of each loin, allowing sauce to glaze over, about 1 minute.

Dry Rub Pulled Pork

MAKES 3–5 SERVINGS

	smoker pouch (see page 10)
1 (3- to 5-pound)	**pork shoulder roast**
1 recipe	**Steve's Brown Sugar Rub (page 118)**
2 cups	**barbecue sauce, of choice, heated**

Place smoker pouch directly on the fire under the grate and turn to high heat until smoke begins to rise from holes. Reduce heat to medium low.

Rub roast thoroughly with dry rub. Place the roast on upper grill rack, or over a sheet of heavy-duty aluminum foil if the grill only has one level. Close the lid and cook for 15–20 minutes per pound, or until internal temperature reaches 195 degrees, turning roast every 15–20 minutes. Remove from grill to a shallow serving dish and allow to rest for 10–15 minutes.

Using two forks, tear the roast into fine shreds. Add barbecue sauce to shredded meat, or serve separately on the side.

Variation: For a spicier version, use Big Red's Spicy Dry Rub (page 119).

Perfect Rubbed Ribs

MAKES 2–4 SERVINGS

1 to 2 (3- to 4-pound) racks pork ribs or pork spareribs*
1 recipe Steve's Brown Sugar
Rub (page 118)

Peel film off back of ribs by hand, or carefully using a knife. Rub the ribs thoroughly with dry rub and let rest for about 1 hour before grilling.

Preheat grill to medium low.

Place ribs on grill grate out of direct heat, cover with lid, and cook slowly for 30–40 minutes, or until internal temperature reaches 190–200 degrees, turning occasionally.

*To enhance and give ribs a more robust flavor, soak them in Pork and Poultry Brine (page 125) for 1–2 hours before grilling.

Variation: Ask your grocer's meat department to rip (or cut) ribs lengthwise to create bite-size riblets.

Kickin' Mustard Ribs

MAKES 2–4 SERVINGS

1 to 2 (3- to 4-pound) racks	**pork ribs or pork spareribs***
1 cup	**mustard**
¼ cup	**honey**
2 tablespoons	**paprika**
¼ cup	**brown sugar**
1 tablespoon	**garlic powder**
1½ to 2 tablespoons	**cider vinegar**
1 to 2 tablespoons	**chili powder**

Preheat grill to medium low.

Peel film off back of ribs by hand, or carefully using a knife.

In a small bowl, mix together the mustard, honey, paprika, brown sugar, garlic powder, vinegar, and chili powder. Spread sauce evenly over the ribs.

Place ribs on grill grate out of direct heat, cover with lid, and cook slowly for 30–40 minutes, or until internal temperature reaches 190–200 degrees, turning occasionally.

*To enhance and give ribs a more robust flavor, soak them in Pork and Poultry Brine (page 125) for 1–2 hours before grilling.

Boy's-Night-Out Orange Ribs

MAKES 2–4 SERVINGS

1 rack	pork ribs or pork spareribs*
1 recipe	Steve's Brown Sugar Rub (page 118), to taste
½ cup	salsa, of choice
¼ cup	chili sauce
3 tablespoons	orange marmalade

Peel film off back of ribs by hand, or carefully using a knife. Rub the ribs thoroughly with dry rub and let rest for about 1 hour before grilling.

In a small bowl, combine salsa, chili sauce, and marmalade.

Preheat grill to medium low.

Place ribs on grill grate out of direct heat, cover with lid, and cook slowly for 30–40 minutes, or until internal temperature reaches 190–200 degrees, turning occasionally. Baste with sauce during the last 5 minutes of grilling.

Variation: Ask your grocer's meat department to rip (or cut) ribs lengthwise to create bite-size riblets.

Spicy Rubbed Pork Roast

MAKES 4–6 SERVINGS

	smoker pouch (see page 10)
1 (3- to 5-pound)	pork shoulder roast
1 recipe	Big Red's Spicy Dry Rub (page 119)
2 cups	barbecue sauce, of choice, warmed
4 to 6	buns or rolls, of choice

Place smoker pouch directly on the fire under the grate and turn to high heat until smoke begins to rise from holes. Immediately turn heat down to medium low.

Rub roast thoroughly with dry rub and place on upper grill rack, or use a piece of heavy-duty aluminum foil underneath the roast if grill only has one level. Grill for 15–20 minutes per pound, or until the internal temperature reaches 165–180 degrees. Turn roast every 15–20 minutes, until done. Remove from grill and allow to rest for 10–15 minutes.

Using two forks, tear meat into fine shreds. Mix shredded meat with barbecue sauce and serve on buns.

SEAFOOD

Perfectly Grilled Salmon

MAKES 4–6 SERVINGS

1 (2- to 3-pound)	**salmon fillet**
½ cup	**mayonnaise**
2 teaspoons	**lemon juice**
	dried onions, to taste
	fresh or dried dill weed, to taste
	salt and freshly ground pepper, to taste

Preheat grill to medium.

Arrange salmon fillet, skin side down, on a sheet of heavy-duty aluminum foil large enough to completely wrap the fillet.

In a small bowl, combine the mayonnaise and lemon juice and spread over the salmon. Sprinkle dried onions and dill over top. Wrap the foil around the salmon and seal. Place packet on grill grate and cook for 15–20 minutes depending on the thickness of the fillet, or until the flesh flakes easily with a fork and is no longer translucent. Season with salt and pepper.

J.W.'s Cedar Plank Salmon with Brown Sugar Rub

MAKES 3–5 SERVINGS

1 (2- to 3-pound)	salmon fillet
	cedar plank
1 cup	brown sugar
1 teaspoon	salt or seasoning salt
½ teaspoon	freshly ground pepper
¼ cup	olive oil

Soak a cedar plank (try a piece of untreated fence board) in cold water at least 15 minutes. Preheat grill to medium.

Mix together brown sugar, salt, and pepper. Coat salmon with olive oil, then liberally rub mixed dry ingredients into salmon. Place salmon on cedar plank, then put cedar plank directly on grill. Grill 20–30 minutes, or until the flesh flakes easily with a fork and is no longer translucent.

Seattle-Style Salmon

MAKES 4–6 SERVINGS

1 (2- to 3-pound)	salmon fillet
¼ to ½ cup	chopped fresh scallops
1	large sweet onion, peeled and sliced
2	medium yellow squash, diced
1	medium zucchini, diced
1 pound	small red or new potatoes, quartered
½ cup	mayonnaise
2 teaspoons	lemon juice
	salt and freshly ground pepper, to taste
	chopped fresh parsley, for garnish

Preheat grill to medium.

Arrange salmon fillet, skin side down, on a sheet of heavy-duty aluminum foil large enough to wrap the fillet, scallops, and vegetables. Arrange scallops, most of the onion slices, and the squash, zucchini, and potatoes around the salmon.

In a small bowl, combine the mayonnaise and lemon juice and spread over top of salmon. Place remaining onion slices over top of mayonnaise mixture. Wrap the foil around the salmon and vegetables and seal. Place on grill grate and cook for 15–20 minutes depending on the thickness of the fillet, or until the flesh flakes easily with a fork and is no longer translucent. Season with salt and pepper and garnish with parsley to serve.

Basil Shrimp

MAKES 4–6 SERVINGS

2½ tablespoons	olive oil
½ cup	butter, melted and divided
1½	lemons, juiced
3 tablespoons	mustard
2 tablespoons	minced fresh basil
3 cloves	garlic, minced (reserve some for dipping sauce)
2 to 3 pounds	fresh large shrimp, peeled and deveined
	salt and pepper, to taste
4 to 6	metal or bamboo* skewers

Mix together olive oil and ¼ cup melted butter. Then stir in lemon juice, mustard, basil, and garlic. Add shrimp, then toss to coat. Cover and chill 1 hour.

Preheat grill to medium. Remove shrimp from marinade and slide onto skewers.

Lightly oil grate, and arrange skewers on grill. Grill 3–4 minutes, turning every 1–2 minutes, or until done. Combine remaining melted butter and minced garlic for dipping. Season with salt and pepper.

*If you use wooden or bamboo skewers, soak them in water for 30 minutes prior to using so they don't burn.

Parmesan Halibut

MAKES 2–4 SERVINGS

1	medium sweet onion, sliced
2 tablespoons	minced fresh garlic
¼ cup	butter
2 teaspoons	Dijon mustard
2 tablespoons	lemon juice
¼ cup	freshly grated Parmesan cheese
2 to 4 (⅓-pound)	halibut fillets or steaks
	salt and freshly ground pepper, to taste

In a large frying pan, sauté onion and garlic in butter until tender. Add mustard, lemon juice, and cheese. Bring to a low simmer and cook for 3 minutes until cheese has fully melted, stirring to combine. Remove from heat and set aside.

Preheat grill to medium.

Place halibut on a sheet of heavy-duty aluminum foil and top with half of the onion mixture. Place on the grill grate, close the lid, and cook for 5–6 minutes per side, or until flesh flakes easily with a fork. Season with salt and pepper, and top with remaining onion mixture to serve.

Lemon-Cilantro Fish Fillets
MAKES 2–4 SERVINGS

1¹/₂ pounds	salmon, swordfish, or halibut fillets, about ³/₄–1 inch thick
1 teaspoon	salt
¹/₄ teaspoon	freshly ground pepper
¹/₄ cup	butter, melted
1 tablespoon	lemon juice
2 teaspoons	chopped fresh cilantro leaves lemon wedges, to serve

Preheat grill to medium.

Sprinkle fish evenly with salt and pepper and place on a sheet of heavy-duty aluminum foil large enough to completely wrap the fillets.

In a small bowl, mix together the butter, lemon juice, and cilantro and brush about ¹/₄ of the mixture evenly over the fillets. Wrap the foil around the fish and seal. Place on grill grate and cook for 15–20 minutes, or until flesh flakes easily with a fork. Brush fillets 2–3 times during cooking with remaining butter mixture. Serve with lemon wedges.

Crab-Stuffed Mushrooms

MAKES 2–4 SERVINGS

³/₄ pound	**medium fresh whole mushrooms**
1 can (7.5 ounces)	**crabmeat**
4 tablespoons	**breadcrumbs, divided**
2	**eggs, lightly beaten**
2 tablespoons	**mayonnaise**
2 tablespoons	**finely chopped sweet onion**
1 teaspoon	**lemon juice**
¹/₈ teaspoon	**freshly ground pepper**
4 tablespoons	**butter, melted and divided**

Preheat grill to medium.

Remove stems from mushrooms, then brush caps with some melted butter. Drain and flake crabmeat, then combine with 2 tablespoons breadcrumbs, eggs, mayonnaise, onion, lemon juice, pepper, and 2 tablespoons butter in small bowl. Fill each mushroom cap with some of the crab mixture. Combine remaining 2 tablespoons breadcrumbs and 2 tablespoons melted butter, then sprinkle over crab stuffing.

Grill 5–15 minutes over medium heat.

Creamy Crab-Stuffed Mushrooms

MAKES 2–4 SERVINGS

³⁄₄ pound	**fresh mushrooms**
1 package (8 ounces)	**cream cheese, softened**
¹⁄₂ cup	**finely crushed croutons**
¹⁄₄ cup	**Parmesan cheese**
¹⁄₈ teaspoon	**minced fresh garlic**
¹⁄₂ pound	**crabmeat**
	paprika, to taste

Clean mushrooms and remove stems. Mix cream cheese with crushed croutons, Parmesan cheese, and garlic until fluffy. Shred crabmeat and stir into cream cheese mixture. Place a spoonful of mixture into each mushroom cap, then dust with paprika.

Grill 5–15 minutes over medium heat.

Bacon-Wrapped Shrimp

MAKES 4–6 SERVINGS

24	large shrimp, peeled and deveined
12	slices bacon

Preheat grill to medium.

Wrap shrimp with half slice of bacon and secure with a toothpick, or put the bacon-wrapped shrimp on a skewer. Lightly oil grate and place shrimp on grill. Grill 3–4 minutes, turning frequently. When bacon is fully cooked, serve.

Simple White Fish

MAKES 4 SERVINGS

4	halibut or pike fillets
4 tablespoons	butter
3 to 4 teaspoons	fresh marjoram

Preheat grill to medium.

Place individual fish fillets on a piece of aluminum foil. Dot each with 1 tablespoon butter and sprinkle with $\frac{1}{2}$ to 1 teaspoon marjoram. Fold foil tightly over fish. Place on grill 15–20 minutes over medium heat, or until done.

DESSERTS

Just Peachy

MAKES 4 SERVINGS

2	**large peaches**
2 tablespoons	**orange juice**
	brown sugar
	vanilla ice cream or frozen yogurt, to serve

Clean, halve, and pit peaches, then brush with orange juice. Roll peaches in brown sugar, then place them cut side up on grill. Spoon any excess orange juice into centers followed by more brown sugar.

Grill 3–5 minutes, or until sugar is lightly caramelized. Transfer to serving dishes and top with scoop of ice cream or frozen yogurt.

Perfect Pears

MAKES 3–5 SERVINGS

¼ cup	**sugar**
1 tablespoon	**cinnamon**
4	**medium pears, cut into ¼-inch-thick slices**

Preheat grill to medium high.

Mix sugar and cinnamon in a bowl. Cover pear slices with sugar mixture. Grill 5–8 minutes, turning every minute, or until tender.

Grilled Apple Delight

MAKES 3–5 SERVINGS

¼ cup	sugar
1 tablespoon	cinnamon
	nutmeg, to taste
1 tablespoon	oatmeal
¼ cup	brown sugar
4	medium red or golden delicious apples, cut into ¼-inch-thick slices

Preheat grill to medium high.

Mix sugar, cinnamon, nutmeg, oatmeal, and brown sugar in a bowl. Roll apple slices in mixture. Grill 3–4 minutes, turning every minute, or until tender.

#96

Chocolate Banana Bang-a-Rang

MAKES 2 SERVINGS

2	ripe bananas, unpeeled
4 scoops	vanilla ice cream, to serve
4 tablespoons	hot fudge sauce, to serve

Preheat grill to medium high.

Place unpeeled bananas on grill 4–6 minutes, turning frequently until peel is blackened. Remove from grill, then peel and slice bananas lengthwise. Serve topped with vanilla ice cream and hot fudge.

Banana Boats

MAKES 4 SERVINGS

4 **ripe firm bananas**
½ **cup** **chocolate chips**
½ **cup** **miniature marshmallows**

Preheat grill to medium high.

Peel one section of each banana from top to bottom, remove, and discard that section of peel. Following the outline of the remaining peel on the banana, cut out and remove a thin wedge of banana the same shape as the exposed fruit.

Fill the space in the top of each banana with an even mixture of chocolate chips and marshmallows. Place bananas on grill out of direct heat, close the lid, and let cook for 2–3 minutes, or until the chocolate chips start to melt and marshmallows begin to turn golden.

Cinnamon Rolled Snail Snacks

MAKES 2–4 SERVINGS

¼ cup	sugar
1 tablespoon	cinnamon
4 slices	white bread
	butter, softened

Preheat grill to medium.

In a small bowl, mix together the sugar and cinnamon. Trim the crusts from each slice of bread; discard crusts.

Flatten the bread slices slightly with a rolling pin and then spread a thin coat of butter over one side of each piece of bread. Sprinkle the cinnamon and sugar mixture evenly over the buttered side. Roll the bread, with the filling on the inside, into a tight roll; secure with toothpicks that have been soaked in water.

Lay bread rolls across lightly oiled grill grate and cook for 2–3 minutes, turning every minute until lightly toasted. Remove from grill and cut into 1-inch pieces to serve.

#99

Ryan's Tasty Banana Treats
MAKES 2 SERVINGS

2	ripe bananas, unpeeled
1/4 cup	brown sugar
2 teaspoons	cinnamon

Preheat grill to medium high.

Place unpeeled bananas on grill 4–6 minutes, turning frequently until peel is blackened. Remove from grill, then peel and slice bananas into bite-size pieces. Roll in sugar and cinnamon mixture and serve.

#100

Sweet BBQ Pineapple
MAKES 4–6 SERVINGS

1	fresh pineapple, cored and sliced into 1/2-inch-thick slices
1/2 cup	orange juice or apple juice
1/4 cup	brown sugar
1 tablespoon	cinnamon
	vanilla ice cream, to serve

Combine all ingredients except ice cream and place in a shallow dish or large ziplock plastic bag. Marinate 1 hour or overnight; reserve marinade. Preheat grill to medium high. Lightly oil grill. Grill pineapple slices 5–7 minutes per side, or until outside is dry and slightly charred. Serve warm with reserved marinade over vanilla ice cream.

#101

Grilled Cantaloupe

MAKES 4 SERVINGS

1	**large ripe cantaloupe**
½ cup	**sugar**
4 (10- to 12-inch)	**metal or bamboo* skewers**
	vanilla ice cream, to serve, optional

Preheat grill to medium.

Wash and scrub cantaloupe before cutting; pat dry with paper towels. Cut off the top and bottom of the melon and then carefully remove strips of rind by cutting from top to bottom following the curves of the melon. Cut away any remaining green portions. Cut the melon in half and gently scrape out the seeds and pulp with a spoon; discard. Cut each half into even wedges and each wedge into chunks.

Place melon chunks in a large bowl and sprinkle sugar over top; toss to coat. Thread chunks on skewers and lay across lightly oiled grill grate. Cook for 3–4 minutes, or until warmed and grill marks start to appear, turning once during cooking time. Serve warm over ice cream, if desired.

*If you use wooden skewers, soak them in water for 30 minutes prior to using so they don't burn.

SAUCES
&
RUBS

Sweet-and-Saucy BBQ Sauce

MAKES 1½ CUPS

1 cup	ketchup
½ cup	brown sugar
¼ cup	mustard
½ tablespoon	Worcestershire sauce
1 tablespoon	vinegar
½ teaspoon	ground ginger

Mix all ingredients together in a small bowl.

Refrigerate any unused sauce in a covered container.

Steve's Brown Sugar Rub

MAKES ABOUT 1½ CUPS

½ cup	sugar
½ cup	brown sugar
¼ cup	coarse salt
2 tablespoons	freshly ground pepper
2 tablespoons	dried chopped onion
1 tablespoon	paprika
1 tablespoon	garlic salt

Mix all ingredients together in a small bowl. Rub over your favorite cut of meat about 60 minutes prior to grilling.

Store any unused rub in an air-tight container.

Steve's Famous Dry Rub

MAKES ½ CUP

1 tablespoon	coarse salt
1 tablespoon	sugar
1 tablespoon	celery salt
1 tablespoon	brown sugar
1 tablespoon	garlic salt
1 tablespoon	freshly ground pepper
2 tablespoons	paprika

Mix all ingredients together in a small bowl.

Store any unused rub in an air-tight container.

Big Red's Spicy Dry Rub

MAKES 2 ¼ CUPS

½ cup	freshly ground black pepper
½ cup	ground cayenne pepper
1 cup	dark brown sugar
3 tablespoons	salt
1 teaspoon	garlic powder

Mix all ingredients together in a small bowl. Rub over your favorite cut of meat about 60 minutes prior to grilling.

Store any unused rub in an air-tight container.

Jazzed-Up BBQ Sauce

MAKES ABOUT 2 1/2 CUPS

1 bottle (18 ounces)	**barbecue sauce, of choice**

Suggested mix-ins:

1/2 can	**regular cola**
1 tablespoon	**minced garlic**
2 tablespoons	**brown sugar (great with pork)**
1 tablespoon	**honey (great with pork)**
1/2	**sweet onion, finely diced**
1 teaspoon	**liquid smoke**
1 tablespoon	**Worcestershire sauce**
1 tablespoon	**favorite salsa**
1/4 teaspoon	**cayenne pepper**
1/2 teaspoon	**horseradish**

Add barbecue sauce to a medium bowl and mix in any or all of the suggested mix-ins to create your own signature sauce.

Alabama White BBQ Sauce

MAKES 1½ CUPS

1 cup	mayonnaise
½ cup	vinegar (preferably cider)
1 tablespoon	lemon juice
¼ to ½ teaspoon	horseradish or cayenne pepper
1 teaspoon	minced fresh garlic
	salt and freshly ground pepper, to taste

Mix all ingredients together in a small bowl, cover, and place in the refrigerator for at least 8 hours before using. Refrigerate any unused sauce in a covered container.

This sauce is quite thin so it works best to slowly drizzle the sauce over the meat with a large spoon. After drizzling the sauce on the meat, make sure it has time to glaze over, or it will taste rather bitter. Because of this, do not add sauce after taking the meat off of the grill.

Mop Sauce

MAKES ABOUT 2 CUPS

1 cup	**cider vinegar**
2 tablespoons	**salt**
1 tablespoon	**brown sugar**
1 teaspoon	**minced fresh garlic**
1 tablespoon	**dried chopped onion**
1 teaspoon	**horseradish or cayenne pepper**
½ cup	**regular cola or root beer**

Mix all ingredients together in a medium bowl.

Refrigerate any unused sauce in a covered container.

Marinating meat in sauce for about 30 minutes per pound before grilling gives meat a more robust flavor and tenderizes it by breaking down the tough collagen fibers.

Basting meat with the Mop Sauce every 20–30 minutes while cooking will help tenderize it.

Low sugar levels reduce the likelihood of burning this sauce. If you struggle with burning the sauce on the outside of the meat, then reduce the sugar or eliminate it.

Sauce from Scratch

MAKES 2 ¼ CUPS

½ envelope (½ ounce)	dry onion soup mix
½ cup	brown sugar
2 cups	ketchup
½ teaspoon	Worcestershire sauce
1 teaspoon	minced fresh garlic

Mix all ingredients together in a small bowl. Marinate meat in sauce at least 30 minutes before grilling to give meat a more robust flavor.

Fantastic Sauce

MAKES ABOUT 2 ¼ CUPS

½ bottle (18 ounces)	hickory smoke barbecue sauce or steak sauce
1 cup	Dr. Pepper
½ cup	ketchup
2 tablespoons	lemon juice
1 tablespoon	cider vinegar

Mix all ingredients together in a small bowl, cover, and place in the refrigerator for at least 8 hours before using.

Refrigerate any unused sauce in a covered container. This also makes a great dipping sauce, so reserve a small portion and serve on the side.

Honey-Garlic BBQ Sauce

MAKES 2 1/2 CUPS

1 bottle (18 ounces)	barbecue sauce, of choice
1/2 can (12 ounces)	regular cola
1/4 cup	honey
1 to 2 tablespoons	minced fresh garlic

Mix all ingredients together in a small bowl until well combined.

Refrigerate any unused sauce in a covered container.

Island-Style Marinade

MAKES 2 1/2 CUPS

1 cup	soy sauce
1 cup	water
2 cups	brown sugar
1 tablespoon	minced fresh garlic
1 tablespoon	minced fresh ginger
2	fresh lemon or orange slices
2 tablespoons	minced green onion

Mix all ingredients together in a small bowl.

Marinate meat in sauce at least 30 minutes before grilling to give meat a more robust flavor.

Hawaiian Ginger Marinade

MAKES 1¼ CUPS

¼ cup	sugar
¼ cup	soy sauce
¼ cup	vegetable oil
¼ cup	water
2 tablespoons	molasses
2 teaspoons	minced fresh garlic
1 teaspoon	ground ginger
1 teaspoon	dry mustard
1 teaspoon	salt

Combine all ingredients together in a blender until smooth. Pour into a covered container and store in refrigerator until ready to use. Shake before using.

Pork and Poultry Brine

MAKES 1 CUP

1 cup	water
1 tablespoon	kosher salt
1 tablespoon	sugar

Mix all ingredients together in a small bowl. If brining a lot of meat, make enough to cover completely.

Let meat soak in brine for approximately 1 hour per pound.

NOTES

Metric Conversion Chart

VOLUME MEASUREMENTS		WEIGHT MEASUREMENTS		TEMPERATURE CONVERSION	
U.S.	Metric	U.S.	Metric	Fahrenheit	Celsius
1 teaspoon	5 ml	½ ounce	15 g	250	120
1 tablespoon	15 ml	1 ounce	30 g	300	150
¼ cup	60 ml	3 ounces	90 g	325	160
⅓ cup	75 ml	4 ounces	115 g	350	180
½ cup	125 ml	8 ounces	225 g	375	190
⅔ cup	150 ml	12 ounces	350 g	400	200
¾ cup	175 ml	1 pound	450 g	425	220
1 cup	250 ml	2¼ pounds	1 kg	450	230

MORE 101 THINGS® IN THESE
FAVORITES

BACON
BUNDT® PAN
CAKE MIX
CASSEROLE
DUTCH OVEN
GRITS

INSTANT POT®
PICKLE
RAMEN NOODLES
SLOW COOKER
SMOKER
TORTILLA

Each 128 pages, $12.99

Available at bookstores or directly from Gibbs Smith
1.800.835.4993
www.gibbs-smith.com

Gibbs Smith

About the Author

Steve Tillett is the king of backyard BBQ, and has done it all of his life. Growing up, he was even trained to BBQ, as he was the son of a butcher. A podiatric surgeon, Steve spent his postgraduate and medical residency training years in the South and Midwest, where his BBQ style flourished. Over the past couple of decades, he has created a group of recipes in his own backyard that are fun and delicious by any BBQ warrior's standard. Steve currently lives in Portland, Oregon, with his family.